EMBOUCHURE

AKRON SERIES IN POETRY

Titles published since 2012.
For a complete listing of titles published in the series,
go to www.uakron.edu/uapress/poetry.

EMBOUCHURE
EMILIA PHILLIPS

The University of Akron Press
Akron, Ohio

ISBN: 978-1-62922-208-0 (paper)
ISBN: 978-1-62922-214-1 (ePDF)
ISBN: 978-1-62922-215-8 (ePub)

A catalog record for this title is available from the Library of Congress.

∞ The paper used in this publication meets the minimum requirements of ANSI/NISO z39.48–1992 (Permanence of Paper).

Cover image: *Embouchure* by Brian Barker
Cover design by Amy Freels.

Embouchure was designed and typeset in Garamond with Futura titles by Amy Freels and printed on sixty-pound natural and bound by Bookmasters of Ashland, Ohio.

Affordable Learning Initiative
THE UNIVERSITY OF AKRON

Produced in conjunction with the University of Akron Affordable Learning Initiative. More information is available at www.uakron.edu/affordablelearning/.

CONTENTS

Let us go back from the mountain, down to the plain.

—FROM GILGAMESH

Girl, you've got an ass like I've never seen.

—PRINCE

AGE OF BEAUTY

This is not an age of beauty,
I say to the Rite-Aid as I pass a knee-high plastic witch
whose speaker-box laugh is tripped by my calf
breaking the invisible line cast by her motion
sensor. My heart believes it is a muscle

of love, so how do I tell it it is a muscle of blood?

This morning, I found myself
awake before my alarm and felt I'd been betrayed

by someone. My sleep is as thin as a paper bill
backed by black bars that iridesce
indigo in the federal reserve of

dreams. Look, I said to the horse's
head I saw severed and then set on the ground, the soft
tissue of the cheek and crown cleaved with a necropsy
knife until the skull was visible. You look more
horse than the horses

with names and quilted coats in the pasture, grazing, unbothered

by your body in pieces, steaming

against the drizzle. You once had a name
that filled your ears like amphitheaters,
that caused an electrical

spark to bead to your brain. My grief was born
in the wrong time, my grief an old soul, grief re-
incarnate. My grief, once a black-winged

beetle. How I find every excuse to indulge it, like a child
given quarters. In the restaurant, eating alone,

instead of interrogating my own
solitude, I'm nearly undone by the old
woman on her own. The window so filthy,

it won't even reflect her face, which must not be the same
face she sees when she dreams

of herself in the third person.

MY MOTHER CONFESSED I WAS CONCEIVED TO RAVEL'S "BOLÉRO"

And so began the formality
of my embarrassment. The nightly

polishing of the borrowed brass
buttons that open & close

my heart like a soldier's
jacket. In time, I learned

how to tie the blue silk
ampersand (under, over, & in)

at my throat, just below the absence
where a crabapple would have

bobbed if I had swallowed
one in the womb. Now

I wear white gloves when attending
to my worry's tripleting:

what if what   if what if—
I am made of a man who took himself

too seriously, whose naked chest
was an advertisement

for undershirts, & of a woman
who made him a season,

only to despise his storms.
If I had been a boy, my name

would have been *Alexander.*
(If I had been a boy, my father would've excused my behavior.)

Sometimes I fool myself
into believing my eyelids crash

like cymbals when I refuse to
look dead in the mirror, silk blue

in the seemly dawn. Sometimes
I imagine myself with a third leg, pantomimed

with the butt of a rifle, so I can dance
properly in time to the heart's murmured 3/4.

THE CAST, IN ORDER OF APPEARANCE

First it was the midwife whom my father gave a dozen red roses.
And then it was my mother whom my father gave a rootball
        azalea and a shovel.

And then it was my father, with his faint mustache that wouldn't grow.
And then there were the open-faced grandparents, like two sandwiches
        sliced in half. Things were neat then. No one broke

character or diverged from the script.
And then it was the anonymity of strangers, always present. The family
dog, Rocky the cocker who died in the snow.

There had been a cat with my name years before.
But what is legacy to the world's new?

Then there were voices on the radio, the ones for music
and the ones for crime. On the latter: sometimes my father, named *490*.

Then there were other children, some to whom I was related and others I knew
I could kiss, when we got old enough. But I always preferred
        their parents, the shock I hadn't always been

alive. Every now and then,
there was the great aunt who smashed ceramic angels

with a hammer and baked them into the Christmas
dressing. Someone's tooth chipped. Someone wore too much red
        lipstick that smeared on their smile.

There were those whom I later found out weren't real

even if I kept them alive. Then there was the brother who was buried
in his last Halloween costume—Superman.
        At some point, love

interests entered. Mostly red
herrings. To forget them, I opened books and saw some ageless
faces. I met myself again and again

in the mirror, which is the farthest distance one travels

without being with oneself. I wrote obituaries and copied recipes.
I wrote a song in a dream
I later forgot. I wrote love letters sodden with my humid

internal weather, but I never met the postman

at whom the dog barks from the window. I try to keep the curtains
drawn against the sun, and the door? Most of the time I don't answer,
even when there's a knock.

MY FIRST KISS WAS IN A ROOM WHERE THEY POLISH LENSES FOR EYEGLASSES

Against some kind of machinery he said was *for grinding*.
Fourteen and thirteen, those ages of compendious entendre.

And there he was in black slacks, a black shirt, and a black tie
on Christmas Eve. A Judas Priest tee under the whole ensemble.

And his great and deciduous grief? That his mother had ironed the sleeves
of his shadow and then threshed his cowlick while he played

an unpausable game. A sneak with a comb between her teeth.
A true pirate. His hair was parted faultlessly down the middle

like the Red Sea, and it was so black and so full
of gel I couldn't help but think of those pelicans

and seals I saw on the news rescued from a gulf oil
spill that were sudsed in baby pools with a dish detergent

named Dawn by scientists who were only yellow
gloves. And I could taste his cologne before *it* happened—

as if I'd been frenched first by butane, a menthol
cigarette, and Pine Sol, a comorbid smack that knelled *migraine*.

But there was something sweet underneath it all. (I was hopeful
at least.) Something like lemon candy, a lozenge I let dissolve

on my tongue. (A *yes*, unspoken.) It was his family
business—sight, frames, and glass. And, somehow, they had a private chapel

in the back, where I'd been given a communion of a single oyster
cracker and grape juice from concentrate in a waxed paper cup.

I was at the age where I had stopped believing in most
everything, except love. But that wasn't

what it was, even if that's what I wanted. I'd seen his grandfather in commercials
shave off half his beard for a buy-one-pair-get-one-half-price sale.

But what then did I know of loss? And of losing
part of oneself to someone else? That came much later.

(Although I couldn't see it happening as it happened.)
It was there in my eyes, someone said. And then I saw it, yes, in my reflection.

THE FIRST BOY I THOUGHT I LOVED WAS IN A BAND CALLED ROMANTICIDE

after I broke up with him   He used to call me

dumb

as a way of flirting   A man came

uninvited

to the house the other day

and I stood

on the other side of the locked storm

door, the dog a low

growl at my heel   The man pleaded

for me to *open up*

and take

the free gift of laundry detergent

out of his hands

so he could show me what else

he had   My father told me

to always be in a position of leverage, to maintain

a range

of motion so I could always turn

away or into

an assailant's grip and get away   Lately, my husband

has been sleeping

on the sofa and so I've learned

how to

stretch my body out as far as it will

go to the mattress

corners   to take up space and dream

of her

who made strong the wound by honoring

the tender

scar that men are

always reaching out to touch without

asking and asking, *did you*

get that in a cat fight, sweetheart without a question

mark at the end because they don't care

about the answer only

that they define the violence   I was followed by

a car for ten minutes and at a traffic

light the passenger leaned

out his window and yelled, *I'd love*

to pound your cunt to pulp

while my buddy rips your ass

apart   Some mornings when I wake

I think I can

unthink my body, to make it salt or sand—

my head the top

chamber of a halved hourglass

spilling

into the wind, but I'm trying

not to violence

myself as a way to protect   *this*

will make a kind of tongue

should mine be pulled out,

I think while looking at the end

of my soft-worn belt and not at the blue-scarred abdomen

in the mirror in which I dress.

THE ONLY THING I LEARNED FROM WORKING AT AN ITALIAN RESTAURANT FOR THAT ONE WEEK WHEN I WAS EIGHTEEN WAS

how to tie a tie, which I didn't realize I still know
how to do until I slipped from the closet hook

a wide wool one in smoked-cigar brown
with crop-in-hand jockeys

riding thoroughbreds violently
embroidered in electric orange and yellow

and blue and began the over-under
muscular guesswork of a half-practiced

drill until I had a passable knot
at my throat and a mostly straight

hang, except for its lay
on my tits. Yesterday I found a single

black hair between them, in the space
we call *cleavage*. *To cleave* means two

things, near opposites: to follow
wholly or to halve, a word I can hardly say

differently than *have*. I have two
hairs under my left nipple, recent

acquisitions, and another that's sprouted
from the benign mole on my cheek,

which I call fondly my *hag
hair*. For seven years in a row

I went as a witch for Halloween
and relished the putty my mother

thumbed to affect a wart on my nose
before she painted my whole face

green. There's beauty in unfemming,
darlings. The world seams

when I put on one of my dead
grandfather's shirts and button up with a different

hand than I'm used to. Sometimes I sit around
in my strap-on because it's so fucking

cute: blue at the base with a wedding band
of lavender, a pink pink head. Just now, out

the corner of my eye, I catch my reflection.
Maybe see the mirror blushing.

THEY CALLED ME *UNLADYLIKE*

My rat's nest versus my grandmother's liberal spritz
of No More Tangles versus the eighty percent
humidity like breathing through a wet blanket versus
my cap-band sweat and palm spit to back-slick
the way an angel does before visiting the dying
miraculous. Then it was the boys' relaxed fit
and the infield dirt that made mud quick in the glister
on my calves. I slid safe. I slid out. My nickname:
The Hat. What else? I cupped my hand to my damp
armpit to rude the silence flatulent and twirled
my gum on a finger, the flavor green apple.
I didn't offer any to any boy. No Eve, no nonce.
I fell asleep chewing, *cow with its cud*, and woke
nuanced. All sticky stuck, a presexual soft butch
Medusa. Then there was the haircut with my blunt-
nosed scissors, and then the correction outsourced
to my grandmother's beauty parlor where I was
sweetie and *hon* and *a handful*. My mother tried to
glove her cusses in front of me, called a man
who cut her off *dipdong*, and then one
Sunday, I told my father that Joan
Jett looked *rode hard and put up wet*—gold-beaked
parrot of my overhearings. He threatened soap
and a striped backside. I ate with my mouth open.
I ate until I was overfull. I burped in chorus
with my friend Heather who smelled like buttered
rolls in my bed at sleepovers. I did cartwheels
on the occasion of dresses, and I wedded
every unmarried mother in their blame games
of house. I seeded my imagination. I spread my legs
wide as the Colossus of Rhodes wherever I sat.
My heart was as full as the butt pocket
of my jeans I stuffed with my father's old wallet
stuffed with Monopoly money. 100s only. I was a soldier

and a cowboy and a cop. Then my hope took
the bit and was broke on the bra, big enough
at first for my whipped meringue and a little
shadow. Then I rose like dough. And my worth
was an abacus of pearls I was told to sweet-pinky
from *boy* to *girl*. I did everything I was told.
I made myself thin as the edge of a quarter.
My fruity low raisined to shy whisper. I kept my eyes
averted and screamed at spiders. There were men
who requested skirts for quick access. Men
with curled lips who said eating pussy
was for pescatarians. But now, after my patience
went first to salt and then to drought, my belt's as soft
as a rose petal and I let her tie me up with it
so I can't stop her from telling me how
beautiful, how strong, my body is with the whispers
of her hands. I'm trying to remember that I deserve
love like this, that my body isn't unrequited. I am
whatever I want. A woman in a knotted
tie and boxers. Love tells me she loves my cock
because I can take it off whenever we are ready
to redress or sleep, her cheek on my right
breast. In my dream, I am the Colossus
with conquering limbs astride from land
to land, no less an image of a god than a goddess.

A KIND OF SECOND VIRGINITY

Certain desires? I ate them
the way the viable twin opens a little mouth
in its thigh, just below the hip, to swallow

its cell-shadow. One day, a restless itch.
Like a flea bite or tickle of a stray hair.
It's not unlike a tree healing

around shrapnel. Another stitch
has wriggled out of my cheek, four years after
the surgery that made me

look like me again. In my cursive,
lovely and *lonely* look exactly
the same. I have only just noticed.

At the bar before the elevator
before the room with clean
sheets, should I write you a note that reads,

                   you look so lovely
you might read it as *you look so lonely*
but I am here—finally—

with you—finally—in a man's suit
made for a woman's body. Last night, he painted my toes
so red they look black.

But this morning? I look down and startle to see
someone else standing
where I'm standing still.

THAT TIME MY MOTHER AND I WERE PHOTOGRAPHED FOR *WOMAN'S WORLD* MAGAZINE WITH OUR CAT OREO NURSING ON OUR COCKER SPANIEL GINNIE,

my mom made me wear a skirt. My smile, pre-braces—stone-hengey.
She, in brown eyeshadow and lipstick like an advertisement
for the 1990s. The cat had kneaded the dog until she lactated.
An interspecies adoption, they said, *a wholesome family story*.

But Ginnie peed on the floor any time a man came in the room.
She must've been abused before, my mother had told me. I didn't understand
yet. I held myself *like a young lady* for the photo but I longed to slouch and spread
my legs. (My baseball cap tan, my magpie's nest head.) I hid my period

until she found my blood-stained panties in the trash.
It's only natural, she said, holding between her lips a record of ash.

HYPERBOLE IS UNDERRATED

A kid, I caught a cricket in Kelly's garage and shoved it down the front
of her t-shirt. This was an expression
of love, like swear words we practiced mouthing when our mothers'

backs were turned. But I'm more
sorry than you can imagine. To this day, the cricket is her biggest
fear. Mine? Fire while I sleep, lovelessness,

and octopuses. (Loneliness I can master.) The octopus at the fish counter is laid
out on ice like a gray and many-rayed
sun. Sometimes my belly feels full of shook champagne; this means I am

confronting desire. And what is desire
but an anxiety of distance? How near, how far. I am the world's worst
liar, which means I expect forgiveness,

always. A hyperbole-less world means we are too comfortable,
unprepared for our failure. Yesterday,
a grasshopper rode my cart all the way through the natureless

store. No one but me noticed it, not even the cashier who announced
with envy that I'd bought the most beautiful
golden beets she'd ever seen. I'm dying to see you, so I sent a picture.

TO THE BOY I CAUGHT RUMMAGING THROUGH MY PANTY DRAWER DURING MY FIFTEENTH BIRTHDAY PARTY

From you, I learned *naive*
doesn't mean *blameless*. I learned I was supposed to

laugh, call you *perv*
but invite you back.

I was supposed to say you were just
a boy who was doing

what boys did.
Because of you, I only kept

lace-trimmed bikinis and flossy
thongs in black. I began to dress

for the imagination of the general population
who might ask me out

only after thieving

a used pair from the laundry
basket. You taught me

I was only as interesting
as whatever I was

hiding. I kept secrets then,

if only for their revelation.
I made you,

by which I mean all boys,

my priority, my mirror silvered
with your projection,

cliché and porny.
I served you a slice of my cake.

Blow harder, you had said

when it was time to extinguish
the candles and make a wish.

You stuck your finger
in the frosting and held it up

in front of me.
Do you like the taste of buttercream?

you asked and dabbed it
on my upper lip too fast

for me to turn away.
I don't even remember your name

but it must have been something
common

as silence, as an unheeded *no*,
or as someone like you

in the pasts
of the women

I know.

MY CHILDHOOD DOG JESSIE ONCE ATE A BOX OF 120-COUNT CRAYOLAS AND SHAT SPECKLED RAINBOWS FOR A WEEK

I used to think everything had meaning—
and it does.
—MARY RUEFLE

And how was I supposed to
not look for her
leavings like Easter
eggs or mud

pies with sprinkles
in the tall summer
grass? My humor back
then—fast

to ignite, like Vicky
Volvo's backseat
upholstery
when my mother's

cigarette
wind-whipped
out her open
window and back in

through mine.
The little burn
on my thigh
like a tiny camellia,

the blister's
petals angry
as the lie.
Don't show this

to anyone, she said.
They'll think—
they'll think I—
I butterflied

my heart
like a shrimp
over that. And
when I asked

if I could call
my grandmother
about the rainbow
shit, mom said, *Some things*

we just don't
talk about.
I didn't understand
delight

not shared.
Or pain.
Soon, the blister
melted back

into me.
Like joy.
My forgetting—
human, plain.

"YOU SHOULD WRITE A POEM ABOUT THAT,"
THEY SAY

No, I shouldn't   I'm ill-equipped to crack a Korbel bottle on the butt-end
      of every sinking ship   No, I don't need to

torture-'n'-rack that amoebic memory of the time I lost my virginity, which I don't
      remember too clearly anyway—or that day

I got caught picking my nose in the first grade, its trailing flower girls
      petaling *shame, shame*   I don't want

to track how many steps it takes me to reach Chimney Rock, or bookmark every
      page in my Browser History   Believe me some secrets

want to leap from the Golden Gate and heave into the turbid bay, its anonymous
      blue cresting into angels' brief, shorn

wings   I don't keep a good record of all my losses, for casualties,
      remember, are the dead   *and* the injured

No, there's really no place   for my favorite word *landfill* or my old dog
      who used to roll on dead animals   A man

once told me I'm cold *for a woman*   Another said I *don't*
      deserve   No, I couldn't solve the paradox—

how many griefs would I have to remove from my heap of griefs
      until it no longer crushes me?   At a rainy spring

graduation the commencement speaker says *I can't wait to upload*
      my consciousness to the internet   I'm uneasy

with anything that stinks of the Singularity,   of my heartbeat
        becoming prosody   Sometimes I think my doing

is more like *don't*ing   moving always on the great American script
        of interchanges and exits   No, I don't wish to make

more of the mouthful of my mother's cigarettes I gulped from a Diet Rite
        can, the dog with no hair she kept in the spare

room   My poet's coat of arms is a cowbird on a skittish
        lamb   No, thank you I think I'll just lie

down and shut the blinds   Please bring me a sip of water my mouth's dry
        and yet you'd ask me to magnify the sun to fire?

POEM ABOUT DEATH BEGINNING WITH A
HUMBLEBRAG AND ENDING WITH A SHOWER BEER

Today, for once, I did not think of Death. I avoided him like all men
    in public by pretending to read, by putting in

my earbuds to drown out his *I still need you, baby*s with Patsy Cline's
    I go out walkin'. I watched the unglued soles

of his black Converse high tops pass in front of the bathroom stall
    into which I'd retreated when I needed to

decompress from teaching. But I didn't say anything, only fished
    in my purse for a pink clonazepam

that had spilled out into the bottom with all the pennies and single
    sticks of gum. *I have to take*

this, I said when he later approached, and then I *hello*ed into my phone
    although it hadn't rung. I tried to look busy

all day. I answered emails I'd been putting off and I even remembered
    to say *thank you for your patience* instead of *sorry*

for my delay. I invited students into my office to ask about their summer
    breaks, and I heard about a job

pet sitting four dogs, two cats, some Sea-Monkeys, and a snake. I asked
    the student if she had to drop mice by their tails

into the hot tank. They were brown and frozen in bags, with freezer burn
    on their noses. I remembered then

that snakes smell with their tongues, remembered one flick against a glass
    enclosure. I remembered then what it was

like to be kissed by Death—his tongue like an old, limp carrot left too long
    in the crisper drawer. Sometimes, I imagined

sticking it into one of those old-fashioned pencil sharpeners mounted
    on the wall. The sizing guide, the little crank,

the shavings coming out in coils, you know. Once, when we were
    together, Death forgot my birthday. I had

to plan the party and smear the cake with buttercream myself, but Death took all
    the credit. He was often like that. *A man*

of consequence, some would say. He never laid a hand on me, but any time
    I told him he had hurt me he would say, *I don't*

know what you're talking about. I began to think that maybe I was
    making it all up. *Maybe you are*, he said

without moving his lips, and I began to worry he could talk to me
    telepathically. That seems like something

Death could do, I reasoned. But maybe his voice in me was me too.
    It sounded funny after all, a little off, like Bob

Dylan in the late '80s, his voice just starting to turn to wet concrete.
    Most of the time, I don't think

about Death, except when he drunk-texts in the middle of the night
    or happens to run into me buying

milk. Sometimes when we'd *make love*, as he like to call it, I was too drunk
    to say *no*. Sometimes when I was under

him, his sweat dripping off his brow and stinging into my eye, I
    would think about a woman and how she tasted

after we walked around the city for hours, finding every excuse to delay
   returning to the hotel room we could

barely admit we had for reasons we couldn't say aloud, even to one
   another, even though we both knew.

Today was a small triumph. As I said, I didn't think of him at all. But I can't
   say he wasn't there. Isn't still. Here in the muscle

after I've undressed. In the brown bottle at my lips, in my hand on my breast.
   And in the steam I inhale.

MEMENTO DOLORIS

I once saw a bone had broken through the back of a boy's
hand like a marble cannon but jagged, sharp

enough to puncture, Wolverinesque, if he threw
a punch. But he held it close to his chest like a frightened

dove as he walked *one step, one step* into the middle
school office where I'd been sent by my teacher

to deliver a message. He was so polite when he got Mrs.
McIntyre's attention—*excuse me, please, I think my hand is*

broken—and then held it out to her like a cup
spilling water. Another boy had slammed it in the door at the top

of the stairs, but Jeff (that was his name, I'm pretty sure)
couldn't say this then. He wet his lips with his tongue over

and over and kept trying to swallow, his Adam's apple
like a busy elevator in a two-story

building. *Oh, honey*, Mrs. McIntyre said, shaking
her honeycomb of hair. But otherwise no one moved, not for

seconds in which my own hands seemed injected with ice
water, an ache like the knowledge there were bodies

buried in the ground in the cemetery near my house.
Pain is proximity, I was sure. *In* the preposition

of the body. And so, years later, after I said *no*
and after I was ignored, I made myself as distant

from the nerve as possible. My body kept moving
forward. And I was a black balloon

dragging behind it, that would have risen into the sun
if it could, if not for the string tied

around the neck on which was tongued *yes*
in a broken cursive of cooling spit.

DEEP CALLS TO DEEP

Until I reached the paddock
        where the gelding grey

collapsed, back hooves
        clacking like stones to fire,

I didn't know of the melanoma
        buried like a rotten black bulb

in his cheek and neck. I came
        only to see his viscera

tagged and marked, some,
        like the ropey penis, knotted

with tumors metastasized
        from the initial onyx

jewel, sunk in a bucket for later
        jars, a class next fall. The spleen

enlarged to a tumid berry-purple
        from minutes-ago euthanasia. I know

that empathy is just the body's
        twinging, its infinite note held

on *self,* but as I cupped
        the black cancer, so much like

my own, warm and dense
        as hope, I felt that design

held me in belief's cold
       rigor.   No, I felt alone—

among the bio students
       chorusing Wolff's Law,

bone will adapt to loads
       of pressure. Me, in my inappropriate

shoes, cotton flats wet
       from the dewy pasture,

awkward as a severed
       horse's leg twitching

in the grass. My heart
       then remade of muscle.

TO THE YOUNG MAN WHO ALWAYS SAT QUIETLY IN THE BACK OF THE FIRST LITERATURE CLASS I EVER TAUGHT, WHO GAVE ME A POEM COMPARING ME TO A COMMONLY HUNTED BIRD

Pheasant was my breast, my gait.
You might as well have said *game*, said *fair*.

Believe me, I already know well
inadequency is a buckshot

hunger I'll never fill. I didn't need
a reminder that I must stand

in a room full of gazes, some of them
male. My body engendered

fowl by this gendered
foul. When I finally confronted you, all

on my own, spine rigid
as a talon, you said you were *just testing*

me to see if I was *cool*,
to see if I would report you.

I did, but you didn't know.
You didn't know because no one did

anything, except tell me it was my fault
for not establishing

my authority from the get-go, that, *let's be
honest*, I looked so young.

You are the only student I ever
feared. I told tenured professors and chairs

you made me uncomfortable
because of the way your eyes locked

like a missile, and I showed them your scribble
in red ballpoint, the doodle

of a fluffed hen, but back then I was just
an adjunct, a junk job with no

support, and every one
of them led me back into the hall

and said you were likely harm-
less. And because you never did anything

else, they felt confirmed,
I'm sure. But I know better

what harm is, the different ways
a hand can write *violence*

onto a body. One of my
superiors, leaning out of his office

and stroking his mustache, shrugged

his shoulders and let me go
with a final piece of advice:

Just don't let him know you're afraid of him, he said.
Just don't cow.

ONE OF THE FIRST GIRLS ON WHOM I HAD A CRUSH WAS NAMED HOPE

I once believed in god, an intelligent design at least.
But I also believed my youth was for mistakes,

and so I kept a fake journal, in case I was ever called
into the principal's office again to see Mrs. Wood

with her New Balance on the desk, her gray muumuu
slipping back to reveal a bunched ankle-socklet, white

as a symbolic lamb. More unyielding than Saint Peter
at the gate, she, of course, didn't believe in saints. Or girls

having sex. And so I wrote my fiction in bed—
temptations conquered with my boyfriend and not

his bass-player's fingers slipped under my skirt
on the band bus while coming back from

a game, his sweatshirt covering everything
like a well-made plan. But there were other things

I couldn't admit to myself, much less lie about.
She was one of them—Hope. Sometimes I liked to imagine

her as an allegorical figure like Justice or Fortuna,
but, instead of the accoutrements of a cornucopia

and blindfold, her arms would be covered in disappearing
tattoos that constellated the classroom

daydreams of whoever looked upon her, and she'd hold
a radio antenna, a voice for the dark hours.

I bought CDs she liked, Blink-182 and Weezer.
We were friends, I said, and then we weren't

so much when she became popular. And I was jealous
of phantoms; of her copy of *Anna Karenina*,

well-worn and foxed as the image of what could be;
the future like an unattended dance, the one

at which everyone else is. But our school didn't
allow them. One teacher said girls could get pregnant

from dancing, and I remember Hope and I laughing
together, on the way to our next class. If she was a sentence,

she was a question I thought was rhetorical.
But the world really wanted to know the answer.

I WANTED TO BE PATRICK SWAYZE, NOT JENNIFER GREY

My first declared crushes on men
weren't crushes exactly. Envies, more like.

Not that I wanted to be
a man. But I wanted to be

in his place, with arms like that—
nude pantyhose filled with huge

onions. And with those high-waisted pants!
Crawling on the floor toward her,

I'd lip-sync a song I couldn't sing.
Maybe a kissing

stunt double.
(Or else a different story.)

I practiced the lines.
Same way I had the Mulder

action figure
and not the Scully.

SCABS

I spend so much time looking
        at scars in the mirror I sometimes forget about
my scabs—recent, tender. The other
            morning,

when the sun made the third-floor
classroom feel like spring
        had broken like a stick cracked over

a knee, a student scratched her leg until a scab
from some impossible

mosquito
bite ruptured, a darksome blood-burn

sinking
like a spring down into her brie-
white socks where it pinked, spreading. Sometimes I think
        about those lace-
cuffed anklets my grandmother made me

wear with black Mary Janes each Easter—

the way they made me feel
        like Hermes when a breeze
     caught them and fluttered

at my heels. My body has always been pagan
        in its rituals—all blood
and the goat's heads

of its dreams. I once had to sage
a new house in which I move

my superstitions from room to room

    like a broom, dusting

up my blessings. I've learned to leave
    all my doors

unlocked when I'm not home. I've learned
    to leave all my doors

    open to the possibility.

PATHETIC FALLACY

the sap that I am springtime
　　　　　makes me want to reread Virgil's

Georgics while eating *cacio*
　　　　　e pepe with fresh-shelled

peas this morning over coffee I
　　　　　watched a video of spinach

leaves washed of their cellular
　　　　　information and bathed in stem

cells until they became miniature
　　　　　hearts vascular hopes capable

of want to roll down a hill
　　　　　of clover to cold-spoon chrysanthemum

gelato or to stop whenever
　　　　　their phones autocorrect *GPS*

to *god* the sublime is a suspension
　　　　　of disbelief the earth has gotten

sentimental this late in the game
　　　　　with its smells of gasoline

rosemary and woodsmoke the rorschach
　　　　　of vitiligo on my eyes mouth

and throat the ongoing
　　　　　argument between self

and selfhood the recognition
      of the storm the howling

wind I wish I could scream
      into someone else's rain

WHEN THE PHLEBOTOMIST STUCK THE NEEDLE IN ME, I LOOKED AWAY ONLY TO SEE A TV ON WHICH A CHEF WAS INJECTING PORK LOIN WITH MARINADE

In love, I am as effusive as an opened
artery. No, as gravy
on flat china, with nothing, no biscuit or hard-crust
bread, to sop it all up. And when am I not in love?
Or hungry? But in that moment, I was
eaten by dread, my stomach like a potbellied goose
egg rolling in the boil. I chewed my cheek,
sucked my lip until my mouth went wet
again and I could swallow
the thought of being cruel
sinew, a machine of hunger
overseen by a guilt
computer. Bright and glistening maw
with a bitten tongue, purpled
at its suture. When I gave you up,
I ate a lot
of chocolate, the cheap milky kind, and let it dissolve
on my tongue as slow as spring
to come. Sometimes, having a body
feels a lot like being fluent in a written-only
language, something I could never
say with the taut bouquet
in my throat. I once knew a guy covered in tattoos,
from the hairless mounds
of his slender ankles to just beneath his starched shirt
collar, who fainted whenever
he had to give a little vial of red.
The phlebotomist tells me it's always the men
who faint, never the women.
And I believe it. Some boys in my middle school
coughed *cottage cheese* whenever I wore

a skirt. Which was every day.
Their disgust with the body unlimited.
In a private browser, I watch a woman bite
another woman's ass, her stretchmarks inlaid
like mother of pearl. Desire is the blue flame
of the world burning
into my skull. Sometimes I imagine eating
the eyes of men the way some people relish
the eyes of fish. Briny as food
served on poseyed china resurrected from a shipwreck.

THIS BEAUTIFUL THING IS MAKING ME SO DEPRESSED

as if endings didn't

have their beginnings
      in mind, some well-meaning someone says to take it

one day
at a time, so I take it like some heroin-mirror—neatly prescribed.

it's spring, which the sun knows,
which the birds know
because they're all lungs, but there's still this whole

rhetorical question of snow, asked by everything—

The pines, for instance:
How fucking fresh are we?

My boot tread's ice-packed, but the buds still flash
      as if from under a trench-

coat. But, goddammit,
            nothing's enough yet
      everything isn't, if anything.

HAHA-BOOHOO

When I keep crying long
after I've started
laughing my therapist
says it's my body

grieving because I haven't
grieved properly
as if my body has
unfinished

business like defecation
after death but it seems to go on
for hours and hours even
days and I think maybe

crying will never end
the way some people
hiccup and then live
the rest of their lives

sleeping and waking
sleeping
and waking their diaphragms
skipping like a jump

rope a word
I just misspelled
just now before
I corrected it for you dear

reader because I was told
that's what you need
When I was
a kid I thought

damn was spelled
D-A-M-B like *lamb*
and a few years
ago I asked my gynecologist

for an IED so
I wouldn't get
pregnant I wouldn't have
to have...I talk too

much when I get nervous
or when I drink too
much which makes
me nervous

which makes me
drink too
much which I did
the other

night because I saw
someone I hadn't
seen in a long
time and my heart

is like bubblegum
chewed for
the world
record for which I am

crying for
the record
for the record
I'm crying

AT A PARTY A WOMAN INTRODUCED HERSELF
TO ME AS DAWN

and when she asked my name I gave her *Dawn* too. I don't know why, except
I'm often nervous as light at the bottom of a swimming pool—the deep end

where I once dived for a diamond
that turned out to be just a piece of broken bottle, a hard

lemonade. I wanted to be Dawn because I have never felt so full
of light before. Or birds singing. I often catch myself holding

my breath while doing the most ordinary things like quartering
a lemon or tying a red scarf around my throat as if I must

costume my fear of strangulation, by which I mean my fear of a man's hands

exercising their strength. A thumb makes a perfect
bruise, don't you think? I wonder, is patience a concept

available to immortals, or is it their tariff? I miss the world

personified—the *Anemoi* in their four positions, wringing out their lungs
like oranges, which I must eat in abundance in the winter to save my brain from

nibbling the black hook. Once I had a job to which I drove an hour
into the sun. And, then, into the sun home. Since then I've had one rule:

head west in the morning, east in the evening. Before dawn
this morning, voices awakened me—a woman's accusations, a man's defense.

Youfuckedhernoldidn'tbaby.

Before Dawn, I had another name. The body, being made

of flesh, absorbs sound, which is why my heart will give up one day. But here
     it is: still beating
itself to death. For the reason all violence is committed, I guess—

To feel alive. Or just to feel.

PLASTER CAST

At fifteen I went to a Halloween party dressed as an accident—
all of my self-inflicted injuries for which I was famous.

I blacked my eye with paint and dug my old medical boot
out of the closet. I walked like an architect's compass

to the virgin punch and held up my splinted middle finger to anyone
who asked me if I was all right. How fortuitous

a break, I thought, for I'd coveted a chance to give the bird
without getting into trouble. And I gave it

to everyone. This was long before I learned
to tell someone that I loved them

by saying *fuck you* when they hurt
me, sharp and clear as a splinter of glass

weeks after I dropped the wine and swept the past
into a pan. I fell

so often
my mother took me to the doctor

to have my inner ear examined,
but the doctor said there was nothing wrong

with my balance, only my stability.
Wear a brace. Strengthen up

those muscles. He prescribed physical therapy
in which I was taught to lie

on my stomach and stretch out my arms and legs
in front and behind me, a pose called Superman.

I was supposed to pretend, for ten
seconds at a time in ten reps of ten, that I was flying.

But I still fell down. I fell down flights of stairs.
And up them. I fell on flat ground

walking with someone I love. I began to think gravity must affect me
differently, as if it comes in surges. I began to dream

I was flying and someone, anyone, would squint up
at me and shout, *But don't you know*

you're just standing on the ground?
And then my heart, which had acted as a buoy

in the air would lose its buoyancy
and I would plummet

into wakefulness. I would fall down a well
if given the chance. I would fall from a mountainside

called Lookout and seed myself
in the void. I would fall like an empire.

I would fall into a zoo enclosure
with a live tiger

if I leaned too far over the rail
to see better inside. I would be on the news.

For this reason, I never climb ladders
even to save myself from danger's retractable

claws. Even
my arches are falling. Like a great ruin's.

MY OB/GYN SUGGESTS I CONSIDER COSMETIC LABIAPLASTY,

and all I can think about is my mother
       throwing out

in-date food because she wanted something
       else to eat. Even

though we barely had enough. Even
       though moths

the size of fingernails bathed in the pantry
       flour, its moon-

cool dunes in dry shadow, and rose at
       opening

in a cloud of fine, powdered grain bleached
       as the ideal

asshole, their wings in perfect symmetry—
       complete

in dividing. I admit that sometimes I get
       pinched

by my panties' elastic and taffy-twisted when
       he pushes

in, full as a drunken cucumber in monsoon
       season, but

one of my feet is larger than the other. A breast, too.
  And, there's also the modern wing

of my face, newly reconstructed after melanoma
  razed

it down to the skull. *I want to be normal,*
  a friend

says. *Why do I always laugh when someone gets
    hurt, is*

hurting? My doctor insists: *It will be painful,
    but you'll*

appreciate the revision. Rephrases: *Yes, you'd be
    pretty*

*tender, but, soon, you'd forget
    to complain.*

AT HOME ALONE, IN MY UNDERWEAR
AND NEW STRAP-ON

I admit I searched *how to fuck a woman* on the internet—
because my truth came late as my last period

and unsurprising in how it surprised
only me, whom I only really see when I brush my eyelashes

black or button my blue shirt all the way
to the top

in the mirror or, later, as a fleeting translucency
in windows made

silver in the too-bright day.
So, I can be forgiven for not having

known always the habits of my body
language or toward whom I've leaned

whenever she's sat next to me, her body
giving off a little heat, some sweet-

smelling shampoo. The advice: get used to the heft and weight,
do everyday

activities while wearing it, before
using it in bed. I felt it bend a little

against the cabinet
while I did the dishes, the water almost too

hot for my raw hands, and I even hung
a shirt on it as I walked to the closet to put away laundry—

You must think I'm kidding.
But the body has a way of claiming

the imagination is flesh, is looking
glass. By adding to it, I don't mean to suggest

I'm missing something.

IT DOESN'T MATTER WHO YOU ARE OR WHAT YOU DO, SOMETHING IN THE WORLD WILL MAKE A FOOL OF YOU

Mr. Bolton, the girls' health teacher, gave us some advice about what to do
when we got into an inevitable argument with our future

husbands. *Lift up your shirts, girls,*
and flash him your boobs. Apparently, that was the tactic

of Mrs. Bolton,
my geometry teacher, who, earlier that year, had interrupted a lesson on triangles

to turn on the news. We watched the planes crash
again and again on a loop, and I couldn't help

but want to calculate the surface area of all that steel and glass
before it crumbled. Fall was sex and spring was physical

education, and some of the girls told Bolton
they were on their periods

every day, every single one, so they wouldn't have to
do laps around the track. But I did them always, often

alone, while the others watched from the bleachers,
braiding each other's hair or doing homework. I didn't want

him to know when it was or wasn't. I didn't want him to know anything
about my body, but he measured our waists

and weighed us and mock-whispered a secret—
Bench presses will make your breasts more firm.

He made us read *Song of Solomon* to learn
about *intercourse*, and stuck yellow happy faces to our chests

when we played an extra rough game of dodge
ball. He loved his whistle and stroked it like a pet hermit crab.
I refused to undress

in the locker room in front
of the other girls, even though someone called me

a prude, and I averted my eyes whenever a girl lifted her
t-shirt above her head or slipped her Umbros. I was afraid

of what I might find there,
especially desire. And so I shimmied into my skirt

and buttoned my oxford as slowly as I possibly could,
listening to the others

laugh in their single voice
from inside the locked stall I chose.

I USED TO GET BOYS TO KISS ME BY BRAGGING ABOUT MY EMBOUCHURE

I called my silver-plated trumpet *Bella*
because I was uncreative in naming

beauty. I should have called her *Double
Entendre*—a good name for a losing

racehorse or a bar. I sat outside
of Babe's in my running car, unable

for minutes to go inside, which I'd
promised myself: *one beer*, annulled

by thirst, *and done*. I must have tasted
like tarnish. More than once, I scrubbed

the smoke-gray ring kissed on my wasted
lips by the mouthpiece. Bee-stung

after practice, its red color in the blood-swell,
a bruisy penance. And still I was amazed

by my body's suddenness, its prodigal
repossession when I kissed her black lace

suggestion, and her back bridged
the who I was with the who I am, small

twins disguised in rejection of their ridded
other. I gave myself dimples, bragged that all

those staccato triplets gave me a quick
tongue. I was second chair; the boy in first

told me once that he'd never masturbated
because God was always watching—

I wanted to ruin him. No one was
that good. He would judge me

if only he knew everything
I ever wanted. Which is why I also wanted

to ruin myself. My only weapon
was denial. My only ammunition,

my body. My beautiful, beautiful
body that didn't know yet

how to contain itself.

SOME SENTENCES NEED TO BE WRITTEN IN THE PASSIVE VOICE

Once, when I thought I was dying, I lived
next to gunshots on Saturday mornings. A neighbor's

practice on cameo targets. I'd pull the dogs inside by their collars.
And I'd read or half-read or pretend to and think
about walking out

into the line of fire. Sometimes the brain's funny like that—
you pick up a can thinking it's cola, too sweet and maybe a little flat,
only to wind up with a mouthful of your mother's cigarette

butts. Half my life has been a bait
and switch. And my body, the biggest worm.

Once, I wasn't and still was.
Later, I wanted something, which was an improvement.

I wanted to make love to a woman, but there was only a man.
I laid still beneath him like a trap door

that didn't want to spring. And then she told me I made her dizzy
and I became a —

(That's when I realized the tongue and heart are the strongest
muscles in the human body.)

TO MY FATHER, WHO CLOSED HIS EYES AND RAN TOWARD ME WITH AN OUTSTRETCHED TOWEL WHEN I CAME BACK ON THE BEACH AT MOBILE UNAWARE ONE OF MY NEW BOOBS HAD SLIPPED MY BIKINI TRIANGLE

It was a big one that knocked me under.
And I swallowed it, the whole wave.

Maybe the whole oil-slick Gulf.
But I gave it all back like a fish I didn't need

to eat. I threw up
all that salted green. Some other

people saw, I'm afraid.
And I'm embarrassed. I'm sorry

but, lately, my heart feels
like an algae

bloom, all mushy and green and too
much. (This is something

I can never tell you.)
Last night you asked me

what was wrong—
but I hardly knew

and hardly know now.
It's just that my friend you let me bring along

kissed Jonathan,
my cousin, your nephew—

you know.
I didn't like it and I can't

say why. It's just that my cheeks
have since been all hot and sore

like they're sunburnt,
and, as she told me, I felt like I was trying to swallow

a jellyfish that wouldn't go
down, that was stinging

my throat and the little bell
that hangs back there

and only rings when you scream.
I want her

to go home
or maybe I want

something else
from her. I came out

of the water because it's getting
too rough. Is it supposed to

storm? Have I done something
wrong? I feel exposed.

I wish I could know
you will always rush

toward me and wrap me
in a sun-warmed towel

whenever I emerge honestly,
all of myself.

I TRIED TO WRITE A POEM CALLED "IMPOSTOR SYNDROME" AND FAILED

The way that the sea fails

to drown itself every day. And entendre alludes all those not listening.

The way unfertilized chicken eggs fail to have imagination,
        dozened out in their cardboard trays,

by which I mean they will never break
        open

from the inside. The way my imagination (*née* anxiety) has
        bad brakes and a need

to stop sometimes. The way I didn't believe

it when he told me we were going to crash into the car idling
        at a red light

ahead of us. To know our future like that seemed unlikely.
        But to have time to tell me?

—Nearly impossible. I may have broken
        several ribs that day

but I will never know for sure. *I'm okay,*

I guessed aloud to the paramedic. *It doesn't matter*
        if you're broken if you're broke,

I moaned in bed that night, after several glasses
        of cheap red. I thought it would make a good blues

refrain. I made myself
laugh and so I made myself hurt—

Memoirs by Emilia Phillips, goes the joke.

A friend of mine competes in beard and mustache tournaments,
even though she can't grow one herself—

Once, she donned a Santa Claus made entirely out of hot-glued tampons.

It was as white as the spots in memories I doubt.

The first woman
I kissed who had never kissed a woman before

couldn't get over how soft my face is,
even the scar. Once,

a famous poet said *what's this* and touched my face
without asking—

his thumb like a cat's tongue on the old wound.

He must have thought he was giving
me a blessing.

AT ELEVEN, I DESCRIBED AN AGING, FEMALE CELEBRITY TO MY FATHER AS LOOKING "RODE HARD AND PUT UP WET"

I thought I was talking about horses.
I mean, I thought my mother had been

talking about horses. The way they sweat
when you ride them hard—that oily sheen

on their coats like curing cast iron.
I wanted a horse so bad I checked out

the newspaper during library time,
copying the classifieds onto the back

of my hand: *Gelding, 11yo, 15.5 hands.*
On Sundays, his day

of custody, my father sometimes took me
to a nearby farm to ride

and there, on the back
of Ariel or Carlos or Nan,

I'd imagine myself on my future
ranch with my husband Brian

Oakes, the boy who sat two rows
away and whose father taught us

how to balance a checkbook
during one Junior Achievement

lesson. When I said what I said,
my father threatened soap.

And then he threatened
my mother. He said, *Parrot,*

into the phone. He said, *Just like.*
I was also fat. And Brian knew it.

My father knew it and said,
More exercise or else—

I did Jump Rope for Heart.
The Presidential Fitness Test.

My Republican father, a "McCain man,"
did a Bill Clinton impersonation

as we drove the twelve hours
to Florida: *I did not*

have sexual relations
with that woman. I heard

she was fat. I heard, *Out*
of all the women,

from women. My mother
included. And me, then.

I'm sorry, Monica.
I'm sorry, Joan Jett—

I thought I was talking
about horses.

I thought beauty ran wild
somewhere else.

POPPIES AND FIELD FLOWERS

I know for now I'm alive
from the rock in my shoe, its tender *but*
in my arch built high for

collapsing. I know it from the synesthetic
achoo rumored to be one-eighth
of an orgasm, my nipples tart as lemon

seeds. I carry around
this feeling we're the unlucky
apes who need

clothes. I carry around this want to lie down
among the poppies and field flowers without
crushing them. My need-tos pulse like an ache

in a bad tooth. When I eat six ounces of flank
steak, I consume 497 gallons of water, 90 acres
of grass six times over, and udders upon

udders of a mother heifer's milk, and all their days
alive in sun or rain. I've heard the stories
of survivors drinking their own urine

before lying back and dying, sucking a stamen
of blood from a pricked
hand. I rush my heart along from moment

to moment like a broom, the dust-up
making me sneeze. Every day
is a struggle with the holy trinity

of caffeine, prozac, and sleep—my metabolism
fast as a cave
drip on stone. In the early morning at a recent friend's,

I try to make as little sound
as possible so I don't
wake them, but always when I'm trying to be

careful and quiet, I make the most noise—
stubbing my toe and shattering a glass
to pieces on the floor.

I AM ALIVE TODAY BECAUSE OF THE TREE IN FRONT OF MY BEDROOM WINDOW

Without it, the teenager would have—

Her mother's silver sedan, borrowed for the party, would—

Without it, the wall with its window and against it, my twin bed—

My body, and my legs—

wound round in my sheet, white flannel with blue
chrysanthemums. My mouth a little

open, the pillow wet. Nothing exaggerates like a tree
in full leaf. Nothing lies about safety

like a home. The bark was scarred for years, maybe still is.

I awoke to the windshield breaking
into song. It was that musical—like chimes

falling. Glass sequined the grass
like dew, caught red in the whirling. I watched
from my window while they cut her out,

although my mother told me not to.

The steering wheel held the girl's body
upright while the emergency
workers shined their flashlights into the wreck—

she became so bright she became faceless.

And her moan rose and fell like the sound of the sea.
And I leaned my forehead against the window when I got too sleepy
to keep my head

up. Something hard and unyielding perhaps
saved us both. But, years later, I would kiss a boy with the last

name of Lamb in that same house, in that same room.
Neither of us wanted to, but we'd been sentenced

to our seven minutes. And I thought then, silly me, with a name like that,

he might be gentle. Or something like it.

THE ANTS WEIGH MORE THAN THE ELEPHANTS

this morning I almost walked out
of my house without

putting anything on because I was thinking
too hard about what I don't know

anymore and later I scribbled a note
AC is on—don't break window

when I left the dog in the parked car
in the sun to run into the store

there a man told a boy *only one*
bag of chips or else I'll do your dome

in   I want to believe this was a joke I want
to believe no one's laughing

if it is   when I was ten or eleven my mother
wouldn't unlock the car door

until I answered a question we were outside
Taco Bell it was summer

and she said *I need you to tell me*
something   do you like girls

or boys   and I wasn't embarrassed
I just laughed and asked *why*

are you asking   your face's so serious
I wish I could just pass off the hard

questions like that still   I wish I didn't wake up
in the middle of the night

sometimes a pot boiling over over a thought
of something I did five six

seven years ago I'll tell you the truth now
I once cried because someone touched

my shoulder but I've never cried not once
not ever because I was kissed

CONFIRMATION BIAS

In the bleach-blue light of
      morning, the reason to

stay in bed. In the glass
      dropped by the diffident

hand opening on its own
      accord, a one-word horoscope

of *nope*. In the Muzak
      playing while you wait

in the yawning
      line to order your dark

roast with cream, in that
      sibylline satellite

radio, nostalgia's anti-
      gravity—the Buzz

Aldrin of your heart
      planting flags that don't

wave. In the dream,
      a prophecy of more

dreams. In the crows,
      Take-take-take. In the way

one word breaks
      into another like a wave,

something you didn't want
        to say, even though you've

thought it before. In the TV's blue,
        in the sun, the fluorescents

at work: *you, you*. Light's
        always lifting dark's

rock to find you wriggling
        there, worm, under

the eye, as if that's what you were
        looking for. As if it was

the last thing you
        wanted to find.

WISH AGAINST CHEKHOV'S GUN

There were years when every store at which I worked
was robbed at gunpoint

right after I quit. First, the smoothie shop
for its petty cash, while its crates and crates of bananas

still turned black, to sugar-mush and gnats.
Later, it was a café where my old manager was told to wait

in the walk-in freezer
with trays of blueberry muffins and crumb cake

wrapped individually,
after he unlocked the safe.

After that?
It was worse—a shooting after close.

A guy chased another right to the door
before he unloaded

a clip into the broad back. The morning
baristas had to wash blood from the windows

before they could open.
That was when I learned an owner is always responsible

for cleaning up a crime
scene on their property, even if they're the victim.

What's strange is that,
after I heard, I couldn't imagine the blood

as red, catching the light that deep.
I could only see it as gold

leaf, a little too holy.
All surface sheen.

At that job, there had been a day
when every latte was mismade and every customer complained

and the guy with whom I was working
argued with everyone, said customers didn't say

what they said when they ordered,
so I sent him on break.

He wadded up his green
apron and paced outside, smoking

a cigarette. I watched him
through the glass. I could see almost nothing

else. And then, when a new customer approached,
he pulled up his shirt

and pulled from his waistband a handgun,
which he later told the cops

was only a BB made
to look like the real thing.

We had misunderstood,
he said. We didn't know how to take

a joke, he said. He was just a nice guy
blowing off some steam.

I HAVE ANXIETY ABOUT ANXIETY

Listen, said the hem of my right pantleg.
I might unravel unless you worry

I might unravel.   So this was my long-term
strategy for keeping planes airborne: a slipstream

of possible outcomes. And after the worst?
The afterlife, two choices: lightning held

in the body forever or else a mouthful of milk
curd. But, now, my heart says nothing

except   *too much, too much*
when the nurse listens with her little finger,

eyes on her watch. Every bit of news is carried
on the backs of invisible pack animals—

I feel the donkey-kick turn my breasts
to smooshed eggplant. I worry about

my worry. I revise it like a web.
Which means I have to thread

it over, doubly complicated. *Excuse me*,
said the fire that had not started, some time

in the middle of the night. *Well, here we are
again*, I said to the dark, to the smell

of smoke I invited in from the cold
of memory. A fire that's never been started

is the hardest to put out. Sometimes I drink
a whole French press and wonder why

I'm sweating incessantly. Maybe the cancer's
returned or else you'll stop loving

me. Sometimes I imagine the inside
of my body like the interior

of a fable: my heart's a cocoon
and its night moth can't break free.

MY DOG REFUSED TO GO NEAR THE DEAD RABBIT
IN THE BACKYARD

after he got its smell. Brown like a toasted almond, with no
snapped neck or saliva

slick in its fur. Totally perfect. Except for the fact it was dead.

And so I suspected a heart
attack or a clot that had exploded into its brain like a bubble

in a lava lamp. The dog tucked his tail and watched from behind

my legs as I toed an ear
and then the whiskers, marveling at how they bent and how I could feel

only the slightest

resistance. I've had other dogs who would have killed
anything that moved across the yard

if they could catch it, and another who would have rolled

all over any rot stink, a smell that would revel in her wake even after
several hose baths, a sheen of almond oil.

Like all humans who have ever been shamed

by a belief or boys,
I have a hard time forgiving instinct.

By which I mean to say, the body.

Mine especially,
which I see in everything. The dead rabbit.

The dog, cowed and anxious.

Once, at thirteen, I laid facedown on the floor
where another girl straddled me to draw a dragon across my shoulders

with a green Magic Marker I tried not to imagine was anything other

than what it was
scaling up my back, wet and cold.

BUTTERFLY-SHAPED ORGAN

Somehow, walking through
the clover, I caught a bee

between my big toe and sandal,
and now my toe's full

of sting. Have you ever
put your weight on something

swollen? It's like you've placed
an unburstable grape

between your body
and the floor. The landfills,

I'm told, are filling
with used pens and tampons—

another argument
someone will use to say that all those

who have periods, regardless
of gender, belong

to silences
and shame. My mother's kept the name

of her third ex-husband
who raped

a thirteen-year-old girl
and went to prison

but got out before the end
of his sentence. I spoke

to him only once,
an exchange in which he threatened

to kill me if I ever
called my mother *my mother*

again. I have been orphaned
and unorphaned

by the years, which crowd
and move against

one another like the insistence
of teeth in a small

mouth. My body is
its own prosecutor

and defense, a one-woman
court where every charge is

denied or trumped up
by guilt. All mirrors do

is show us how we think
others see us, but I want one

that shows me only
how I see myself. This butterfly-

shaped organ in
my throat has handed in its

two weeks' notice
but I won't let it go.

I wonder what lives
my gallbladder and tumor are

living, reborn again
by freedom and bloodless

decay. Sometimes I think pain
is the only language

all humans share, but then a male
doctor tells me

I'm just exaggerating
the scale.

BLOODWORK

This morning
my period arrives late
and sludgy. Ten years ago, I gave

birth to a bundle
of cells in the bathtub in the cement
block house—too early to have

known I was pregnant, too
young to feel relief. I carried
the miscarriage all night in gasps

between the tub and the mattress
we kept
on the floor. I buried

the sound of blanks
in my ear, some figurative
weapon raw

with desire. Whenever
I smell red
wine, I'm back on my knees

for communion, the church
always making me
think of sin, the position

my body found in the pew
after service while I listened to
my mother's footsteps

echo in the nave as she refilled the altar
vases with tap water
and then drank the rest of the consecrated

wine that couldn't be poured
down the drain. Yesterday,
without my glasses on, I saw a clothesline

from the car and saw prayer
flags. I want to belong
to some ritual of muscle, but not religion—

I'm genetically prone to high
hemoglobin, colonialism, and paranoid
depression with obsessive

tendencies. Somewhere in the dusty
filings of the state
of Tennessee are the names

of my mother's biological
parents: her mother unmarried,
her father already

with another family. Someday
I'll have to contend
with the fact that my body is a dead language

euphemized by razors
and denial. Tell me again why I should rise and dress
in the name of my father?

MY NEIGHBOR'S WORKING OUT TO CHRISTIAN POP
MUSIC IN HER FRONT YARD DURING A PANDEMIC

Squats for Jesus. Lunges.
Something about capital-H *His*
righteousness. Pit stains on her
Mickey Mouse shirt. Leggings
tight as sausage casings. Her arms—
a medieval-knight sculpture's.

(She waves, jogging in place,
and yells, *Have a blessed day!*)

My dog pissing on the irises.

The birds' songs like a spring bouquet
to which I'm allergic.
Everything loud as animous praise.
Everything lonely as an unacknowledged saint
whose sweat and tears remained

uncollected in any one heart's
four reliquaries.

I THINK ABOUT THE TIME MY WEATHER RADIO FORECASTED "ALTHOUGH THE SKY WILL BE OVERCAST YOUR HOUSE WILL STILL BE FILLED WITH LIGHT"

almost every day, even though it was over
four years ago, when I thought I was dying. The moment it happened,

I almost couldn't believe it had
happened. I was wrist deep in dirty dishwater and wondering

when the snow's rumor would snuff the barelyflame

of my hope. I've always liked how the brimstone's bannermen gave hellfire
tongues but no mouths.
How do you feed something like that? Where does it contain

its vacancy
called *hunger*? Listen, back then, I couldn't not hear this forecast

as a blessing. But now, I think it must have been a prank, a hoax.
A bored intern

taking a poetry class that semester
or a sleepless temp who confused the task of the National Weather
Service data entry with that of her other job,
part-time at a suicide hotline.

Once, I visited the cave that was supposedly Dante's
inspiration for the exit of the Inferno. (Note: it had collapsed.)

And, once, I saw a crumbling fresco of the *danse*
macabre and realized then
that the parade neither arrives nor ends. I listened

to the weather three times over but never heard the announcement again.
But, this morning, I felt a tickle

on my cheek where the scar is, and raised my hand
to rub the spot, only to find a stitch working its way out

like a whisker. The last
surgery, the one where I was remade in my own image, was over
three years ago.

And that stitch, I was sure it was meant to dissolve.

NOTES

The book's epigraphs come from *Gilgamesh* as translated by David Ferry and Prince's "Little Red Corvette" from his album *1999*.

The Mary Ruefle epigraph on page 24 is from her poem "Nixie" from *Dunce* (Wave Books, 2019).

Thanks to Chen Chen for the prompt that allowed me to write "My OB/GYN Suggests I Consider Cosmetic Labiaplasty."

"It doesn't matter who you are or what you do, something in the world will make a fool of you" takes its title from Angel Olsen's song "Intern" from her album *My Woman*.

"Poppies and Field Flowers" is for Joey Kingsley.

Song lyrics from Fiona Apple title "The Ants Weigh More Than the Elephants" (from her song "Left Alone").

ACKNOWLEDGMENTS

Many thanks to the literary publications that first published these poems—

THE ADROIT JOURNAL
> "THE FIRST BOY I THOUGHT I LOVED WAS IN A BAND CALLED ROMANTICIDE," "ONE OF THE FIRST GIRLS ON WHOM I HAD A CRUSH WAS NAMED HOPE," AND "POEM ABOUT DEATH BEGINNING WITH A HUMBLEBRAG AND ENDING WITH A SHOWER BEER"

AMERICAN POETRY REVIEW
> "HAHA-BOOHOO," "POPPIES AND FIELD FLOWERS," AND "SCABS"

THE AUNT FLO PROJECT
> "BLOODWORK"

THE BAFFLER
> "DEEP CALLS TO DEEP"

THE CINCINNATI REVIEW
> "'YOU SHOULD WRITE A POEM ABOUT THAT,' THEY SAY"

THE FAMILIAR WILD
> "MY DOG REFUSED TO GO NEAR THE DEAD RABBIT IN THE BACKYARD"

FOGLIFTER
> "I USED TO GET BOYS TO KISS ME BY BRAGGING ABOUT MY EMBOUCHURE" AND "TO THE BOY I CAUGHT RUMMAGING THROUGH MY PANTY DRAWER DURING MY FIFTEENTH BIRTHDAY PARTY"

GREAT RIVER REVIEW
> "THE CAST, IN ORDER OF APPEARANCE," "HYPERBOLE IS UNDERRATED," "I AM ALIVE TODAY BECAUSE OF THE TREE IN FRONT OF MY BEDROOM WINDOW," AND "PLASTER CAST"

THE GREENSBORO REVIEW
> "CONFIRMATION BIAS"

GRIST
> "MY OB/GYN SUGGESTS I CONSIDER COSMETIC LABIAPLASTY"

GULF COAST

"MEMENTO DOLORIS" AND "THE ONLY THING I LEARNED
WORKING AT AN ITALIAN RESTAURANT FOR THAT ONE WEEK
WHEN I WAS EIGHTEEN WAS"

THE MISSOURI REVIEW POEM OF THE WEEK

"I HAVE ANXIETY ABOUT ANXIETY"

POEM-A-DAY (ACADEMY OF AMERICAN POETS)

"AGE OF BEAUTY," "I TRIED TO WRITE A POEM CALLED
'IMPOSTOR SYNDROME' AND FAILED" AND "PATHETIC
FALLACY"

POETRY INTERNATIONAL

"MY MOTHER CONFESSED I WAS CONCEIVED TO RAVEL'S
'BOLÉRO'"

QUARTERLY WEST

"MY FIRST KISS WAS IN A ROOM WHERE THEY POLISH LENSES
FOR EYEGLASSES," "SOME SENTENCES NEED TO BE WRITTEN
IN THE PASSIVE VOICE," AND "WHEN THE PHLEBOTOMIST
STUCK THE NEEDLE IN ME, I LOOKED AWAY ONLY TO SEE A
TV ON WHICH A CHEF WAS INJECTING PORK LOIN WITH
MARINADE"

RADAR POETRY

"BUTTERFLY-SHAPED ORGAN"

THE RUMPUS

"AT A PARTY A WOMAN INTRODUCED HERSELF TO ME AS
DAWN," "DOESN'T MATTER WHO YOU ARE OR WHAT YOU DO,
SOMETHING IN THE WORLD WILL MAKE A FOOL OF YOU,"
AND "A KIND OF SECOND VIRGINITY"

THE SOUTHEAST REVIEW

"AT ELEVEN, I DESCRIBED AN AGING, FEMALE CELEBRITY TO
MY FATHER AS LOOKING 'RODE HARD AND PUT UP WET'"
AND "MY CHILDHOOD DOG JESSIE ONCE ATE A BOX OF
120-COUNT CRAYOLAS AND SHAT SPECKLED RAINBOWS FOR
A WEEK"

THE SOUTHERN REVIEW

"TO THE YOUNG MAN WHO ALWAYS SAT QUIETLY IN THE
BACK OF THE FIRST LITERATURE CLASS I EVER TAUGHT,
WHO GAVE ME A POEM COMPARING ME TO A COMMONLY
HUNTED BIRD"

SPORKLET

"I WANTED TO BE PATRICK SWAYZE, NOT JENNIFER GREY"

TINDERBOX POETRY

"THIS BEAUTIFUL THING IS MAKING ME SO DEPRESSED"

—especially to those editors who solicited my work, including Eloisa Amezcua, Peter Campion, Alex Dimitrov, Nicole Terez Dutton, Caitlin Doyle, Katie Condon, and Lauren Hilger.

Many thanks to Jenny Browne, Sumita Chakraborty, Oliver de la Paz, Matthew Guenette, Rebecca Hazelton, Sara Eliza Johnson, Erika Meitner, and Lena Moses-Schmitt, all members of the 2017 and 2018 Blob-a-Day groups who held me accountable and kept me encouraged while I drafted many of these poems. Special thanks to Oliver and Erika for continuing the accountability in autumn 2018.

Many thanks to the Sundress Academy of the Arts and their Firefly Farms for giving me the space in summer 2017 to think about and chisel away at this collection. Endless gratitude to Can Serrat Artists' Residency for the space to allow me to write several of these poems.

To those who read this book and its poems in its manuscript forms, thank you: Erin Andersen, Rebecca Hazelton, Joey Kingsley, Rachel Mennies, Jessica Morey-Collins, Lena Moses-Schmitt, and Anna Sutton.

To my editor Mary Biddinger and book designer Amy Freels: thank you for making this a real book.

Thank you to my colleagues at University of North Carolina at Greensboro, especially the creative writing faculty, current and retired: Stuart Dischell, Terry Kennedy, Jessie Van Rheenan, Holly Goddard Jones, Michael Parker, Craig Nova, Xhenet Aliu, and Derek Palacio. Thank you also to UNCG's English Department and the Women's, Gender, and Sexuality Studies Department.

Thank you to my students: our conversations have changed the DNA of my poems.

Thank you to those people, organizations, and businesses who make up my local community, especially Scuppernong Books. Brian and Steve, I'm ready for my "named chair," that mustard-colored velour one in the event space.

Thank you and love to those friends and family who supported me endlessly when I came out, especially my mother Janet; stepmother Sonia; friends Gregory, Tracy, and others already mentioned here.

Much gratitude to F. and E. for your support and community. And, lastly: Te amo, C. Nosotras juntas.

Emilia Phillips (she/they) is the author of four poetry collections from the University of Akron Press and four chapbooks. Winner of a 2019 Pushcart Prize and a 2019–2020 NC Arts Council Fellowship, Phillips's poems, lyric essays, and book reviews appear widely in literary publications including *Agni, American Poetry Review, Gulf Coast, The Kenyon Review, New England Review, The New York Times, Ploughshares,* and elsewhere. She's a faculty member of the MFA Writing Program and Department of English and cross-listed faculty with the Women's, Gender, and Sexuality Studies Program at UNC Greensboro.

Printed in the United States
By Bookmasters